Text and illustration copyright © 2016
by Princess Ivana Pignatelli, Magdalene Smith, and Marisa Smith

All rights reserved. Except as permitted under the U.S. Copyright Act of 1976, no part of this book may be reproduced, distributed, or transmitted in any form or by any means, or stored in a database or retrieval system, without prior written permission of the copyright holders. Address queries to info@dontsweatitmedia.com.

Don't Sweat It Media, Inc.
First U.S. edition 2016

Illustrations by Hanna Barczyk
Graphic Design by Rima Hawkes

Printed in the United States of America

Library of Congress Control No. 2016902311
ISBN 978-0-692-63805-7

PUBLISHER'S NOTE

Perfectly Awkward Tales are original works by Princess Ivana, Magdalene Smith, and Marisa Smith. Books in the series are *Vasilisa & Intuition, Aila & Determination, Ninetta & Confidence,* and *Color & Creativity.*

www.perfectlyawkwardtales.com

Perfectly Awkward Tales

COLOR & CREATIVITY

Illustrated by
Hanna Barczyk

About the Illustrator

Hanna Barczyk was born in Germany and currently divides her time between New York City and Toronto. She creates conceptual illustrations for major publications such as *The New York Times* and *The Washington Post*, among many others.

Inspired by her family's Hungarian folk art traditions, memories, love, music, movement, and a passion for dance, Hanna's illustrations brim with emotional truth, bold and delicate at the same time.

Hanna has been recognized by the Society of Illustrators, American Illustration, *Creative Quarterly* and *3x3* (Magazine of Contemporary Illustration). She is the recipient of the Melville White Award, and has been the subject of a feature in *Communication Arts Magazine*.

Perfectly Awkward Tales

Girl heroes from around the world discover their hidden gifts in this series of smart, funny and crazy adventures.

Vasilisa & Intuition
Vasilisa is from Russia. She is only ten years old, but must outsmart Baba Yaga, a powerful witch with iron teeth who likes to have children for supper. (Not as a guest, but as the main course!) With the help of her faithful doll, Inti, Vasilisa discovers the power of her gift. Intuition.

Aila & Determination
Aila is from Scotland. She is thirteen years old, an orphan with no one in the world but her baby sister, Maisie. But Maisie has disappeared. Stolen by powerful fairies from the Land of Sidh. When Aila begins the impossible journey to find her, she discovers the power of her gift. Determination.

Ninetta & Confidence
Ninetta is from Italy. She is twelve years old and embarrassed about her strange talents. So embarrassed, she'd rather be invisible! Life is miserable being a weirdo, until Ninetta jumps down a wishing well and finds a magic garden where she feels right at home. But the garden has a secret. Can a weirdo be a hero? Ninetta isn't sure, until she faces greedy King Ransack and discovers the power of her gift. Confidence.

Written by Princess Ivana, Magdalene Smith, and Marisa Smith
Illustrated by Hanna Barczyk

www.perfectlyawkwardtales.com

 Don't Sweat It Media, Inc.

Different is Powerful

To all the perfectly awkward people in this world. Thank you for being you.

    Color & Creativity invites you to play on every page. Jump into the stories with Vasilisa, Aila, and Ninetta. Discover your own hidden talents. There are pages to color, scribble, draw, or tell your own story, any way you want!
    Creativity is a gift we all have. There are no rules. Don't worry about what others think. What matters is what you think. Creativity builds intuition, determination, and confidence. It helps us get in touch with our thoughts and feelings by giving us space to dream.

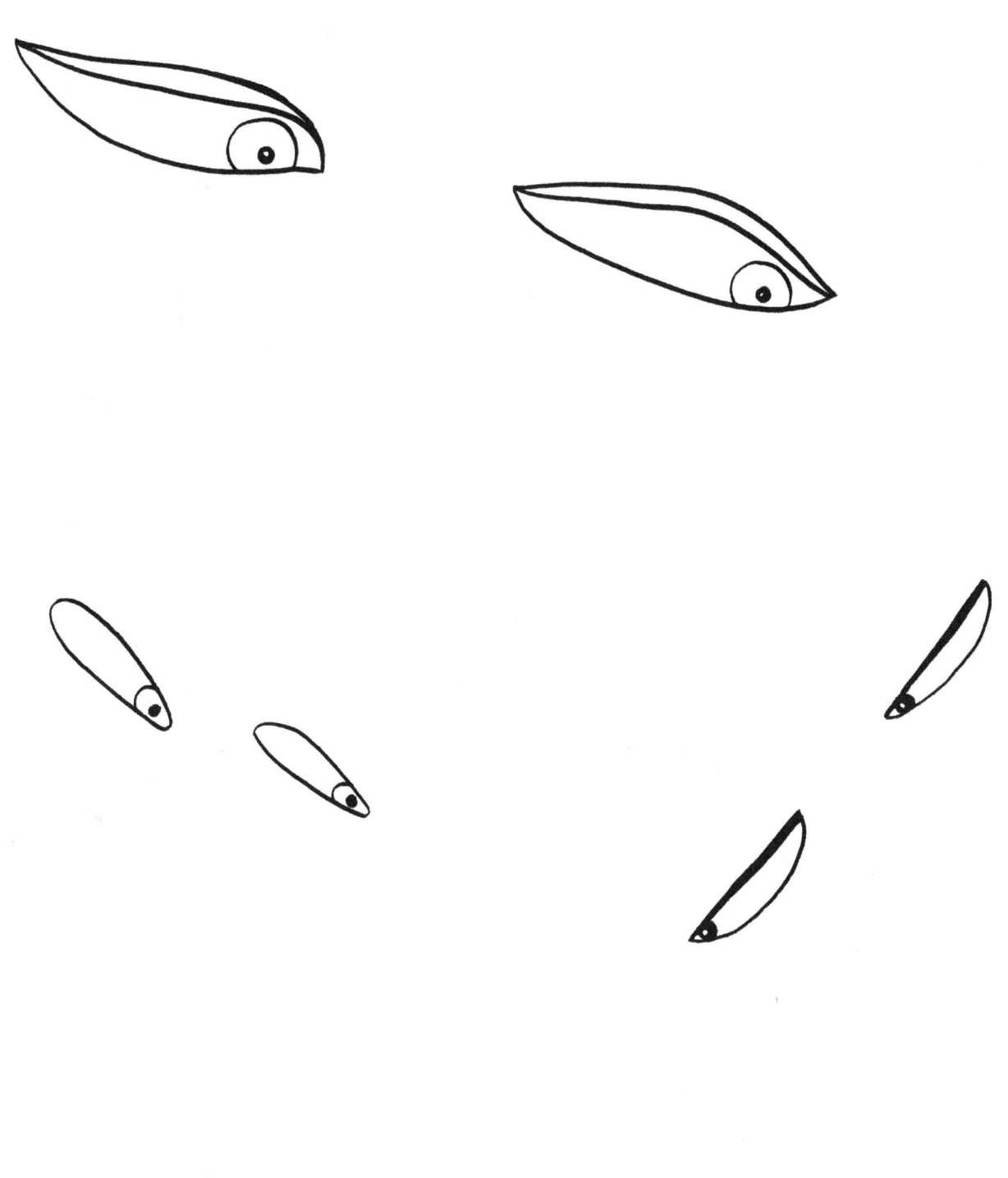

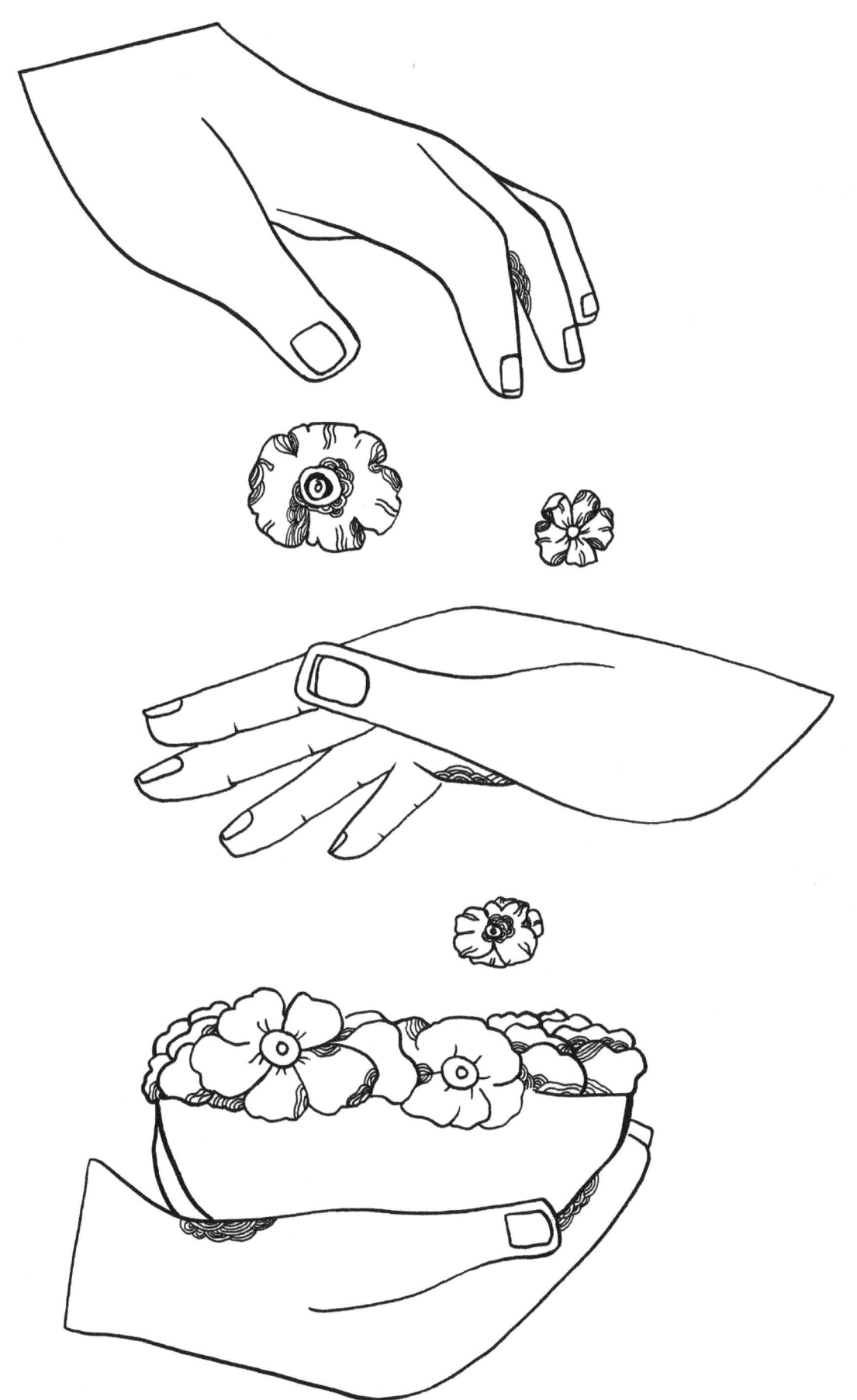

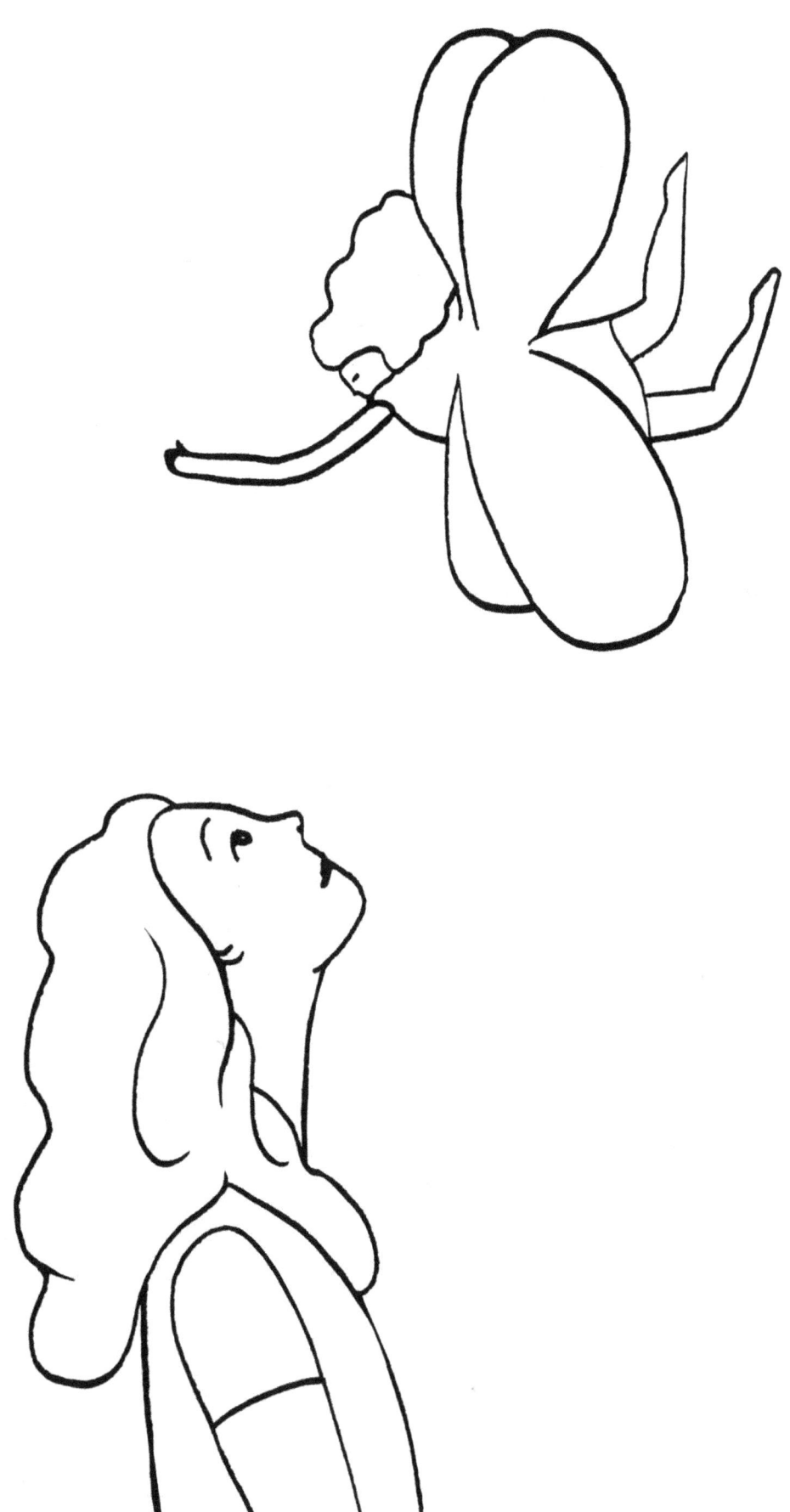

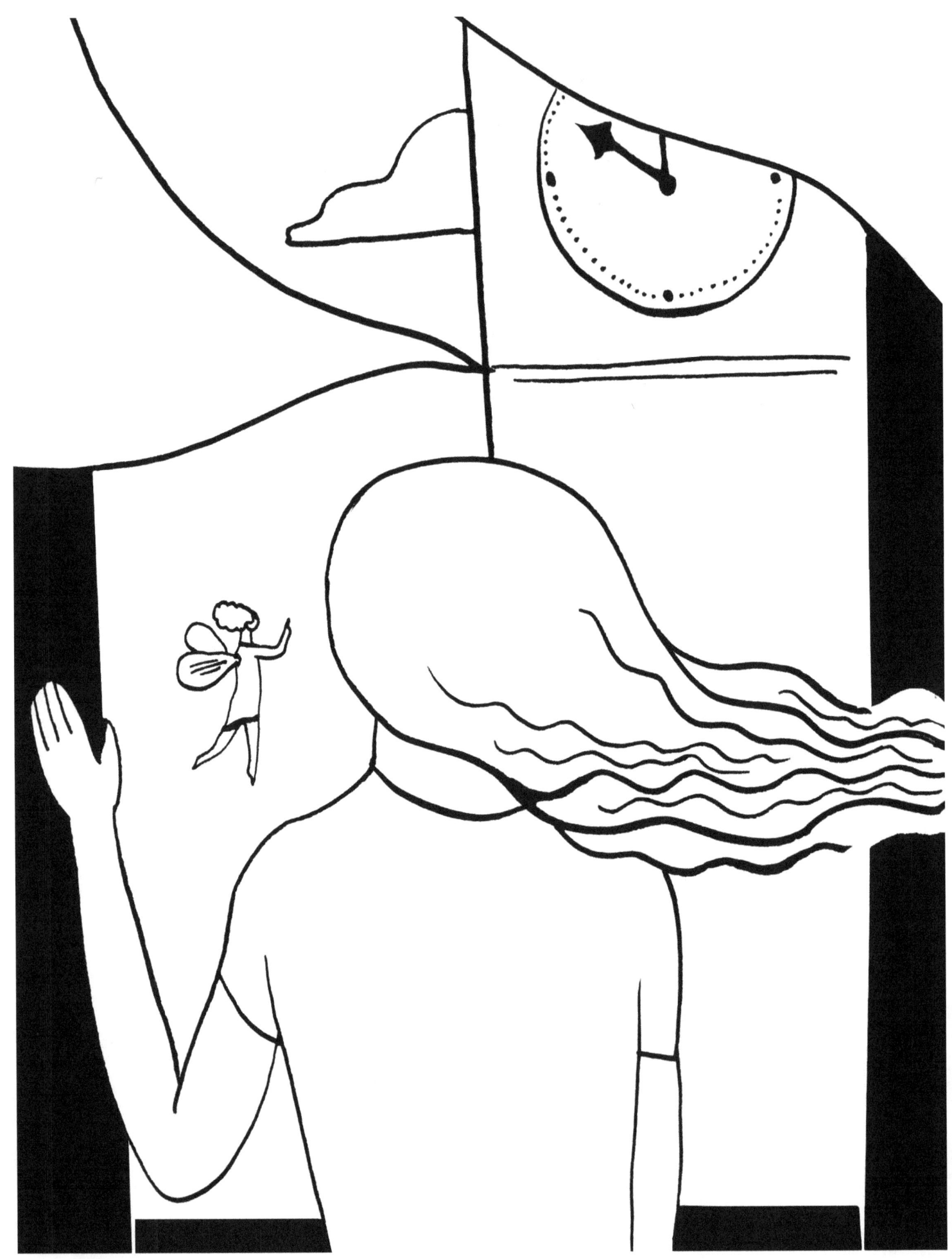

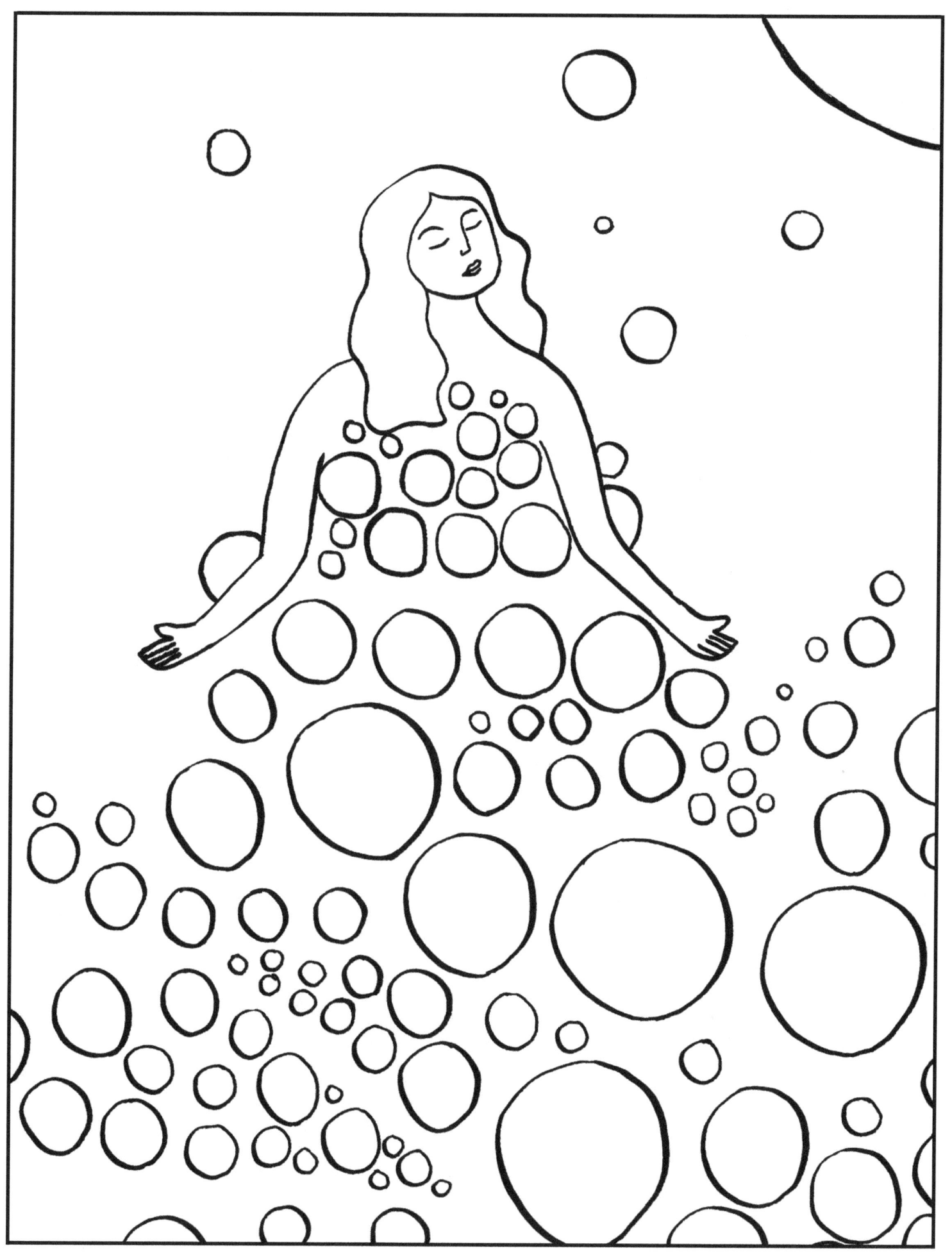

www.ingramcontent.com/pod-product-compliance
Lightning Source LLC
Chambersburg PA
CBHW081459040426
42446CB00016B/3316